LIFE ON A DAIRY FARM

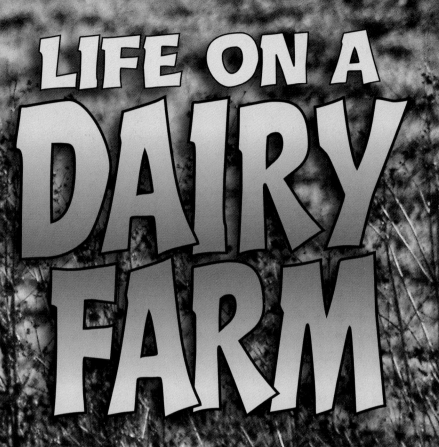

LIFE ON A DAIRY FARM

by Judy Wolfman

photographs by David Lorenz Winston

LIFE ON A FARM

Carolrhoda Books, Inc. / Minneapolis

To Marilyn, Duane, Robert, and Kacie Hershey, for opening our eyes to the ways of raising cows and running a dairy farm. You made our experience a memorable one. Thank you.

—J.W. and D.L.W.

Text copyright © 2004 by Judy Wolfman
Photographs copyright © 2004 by David Lorenz Winston

Carolrhoda Books, Inc.
A division of Lerner Publishing Group
241 First Avenue North
Minneapolis, MN 55401 U.S.A.

Website address: www.lernerbooks.com

Library of Congress Cataloging-in-Publication Data

Wolfman, Judy.
    Life on a dairy farm / by Judy Wolfman ; photographs by David Lorenz
Winston.
        p.   cm. — (Life on a farm)
    Summary: Explains the activities that take place on a working dairy farm,
from the perspective of a child who lives there.
    Includes index.
    ISBN: 1–57505–190–7 (lib. bdg. : alk. paper)
    1. Dairy cattle—Juvenile literature. 2. Cows—Juvenile literature. 3. Dairy
farms—Juvenile literature. 4. Farm life—Juvenile literature. [1. Cows.
2. Dairy farms. 3. Farm life.] I. Winston, David Lorenz, ill. II. Title.
SF208.W65 2004
636.2'142—dc21   2002154719

Manufactured in the United States of America
1 2 3 4 5 6 – JR – 09 08 07 06 05 04

CONTENTS

Our DAIRY Farm Is Ar-Joy

I'm proud of the sign
for my family's farm.

To me, nothing tastes better than a glass of fresh, cold milk that comes from cows! My name is Robert Hershey, and I live with my family on our dairy farm. On a dairy farm, animals are raised to give milk. We milk about 400 cows every day of the year.

Our farm is called the Ar-Joy Dairy Farm. Dad grew up here, so he knows how to raise cows. Mom grew up on a dairy farm, too. Besides my parents, I have two brothers, Steve and Kelby, and one sister, Kacie.

On our farm, we have three silos to store feed for the cows. We fill the silos with corn and chopped hay.

We are the Hershey family!

Living on a dairy farm means lots of work, especially for Dad. He has seven workers to help him out. Their days are long, every day of the week. Dad usually gets up at 5 in the morning and doesn't go to bed until 10 at night. My brothers, sister, and I help him out when we can. During the school year, we do our chores before and after school. But in the summer, we work on the farm during the day.

Even though there's plenty of work to do, we like living on our farm—and we like the cows!

My sister, Kacie, is leading a calf from the pasture to the barn.

All of our cows are Holsteins. Holsteins are the most popular milk cow and give more milk than any other kind. We have 700 Holsteins. Around 400 are cows that give milk, and 300 are **calves** and **heifers**. Calves are baby cows. Heifers are young girl cows that can't give milk yet. To give milk, a cow must first give birth to a calf. Then they'll start giving milk. Did you know that all cows are female? The males are called **bulls**.

When the weather is warm, our cows spend lots of time outside.

Sometimes cows in heat behave strangely. This one is rubbing up against a tree.

When a heifer is about 13 months old, she is usually ready to become pregnant. We can tell when she goes into **heat**. She walks around a lot and pushes other cows around. When we see her do this, we **breed** her, or make her pregnant. To breed a heifer, Dad first takes a special liquid from a bull that can make a female cow pregnant. Then he puts the liquid into her body.

This cow is pregnant. It won't be long before she gives birth to a calf!

Every two weeks, an animal doctor, or **veterinarian**, comes to our farm. He checks the cows to find out if any are pregnant. If a cow is not pregnant, Dad knows he has to try to breed her again. If she is pregnant, we can start to plan for a new calf. When a cow becomes pregnant, she usually carries one baby for nine months.

While we take care of our pregnant cows, we get ready for what will happen next. And what an amazing event it will be!

This pregnant cow is taking a lunch break.

This pregnant cow will give birth very soon!

A

CALF
Is Born

About nine months after a cow becomes pregnant, she gets ready to calve, or have a baby. We can tell she's ready, because she usually fidgets. She stands up and sits down a lot. Her udder gets full with milk. An udder is the part of a cow that makes milk. It looks like a bag and hangs under the cow's belly.

14

After about an hour, she starts to push. It takes about one to two hours of pushing before a calf is born. When it's time, the calf slips out, front feet first. The calf usually has its eyes closed but opens them after a few seconds. The calf is wet with **mucus,** a slippery coating that feels like jelly. The mother licks the mucus off right away. Licking the calf is important—it calms the baby down, and it feels good.

These calves were just born. They're resting before they try to stand up.

Little calves like to be petted. Here I'm playing with two newborns.

Usually a cow has only one calf, but sometimes twins come. We're glad to see girl calves born, since they can give us milk later. If a boy is born, we might sell it to a farmer who needs a bull to breed his cows.

A newborn calf weighs between 80 and 100 pounds. It's about the size of a large dog. A calf is born with its own unique black-and-white markings on its body. Just like fingerprints and snowflakes, each cow's markings are different. It's hard to tell if they are black with white spots, or white with black spots.

After a long day, this newborn calf takes a rest.

It doesn't take long before a calf tries to stand on its own.

Some people are surprised how well our cows and cats get along!

Right after a calf is born, it usually wants to rest for a while. After fifteen or twenty minutes, it tries to stand up. Its back legs straighten up first, then its front legs. Its legs are very wobbly. The calf falls, then gets up again many times. Finally, it stands on all four legs.

After the calf stands, we give it a numbered tag. We attach the tag to the middle of one of its ears. (It doesn't hurt the calf when we do this.) The numbered tags help us keep track of our calves. With the tags on, they look like they're wearing earrings!

By this time, the calf starts to look for milk to drink. Right away, we take the calf from its mother. We do this because we don't want the calf to drink from its mother's **teats,** or nipples. Teats are not always clean, and we don't want the calf to get germs. Germs can make it sick.

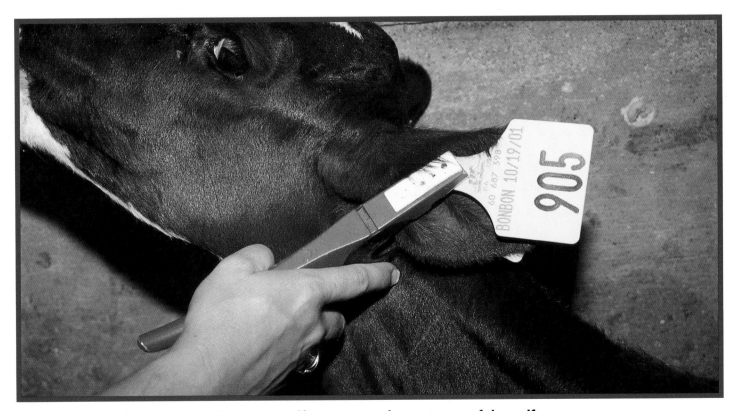

After we attach a numbered tag to a calf's ear, we take a picture of the calf.
That way, we will have a record of the calf's special markings.

After we separate the cow and the calf, we put them in two different barns. In the cow's barn, we milk her right away.

The mother's first milk is called **colostrum**. It has vitamins and minerals that help the calf get a good start.

Look at the size of this bottle! Here we're feeding the calf her mother's colostrum.

This calf is getting used to its new home.

Then we go to the calf's barn and feed her the colostrum in a bottle. (The bottle looks like one that's used to feed a human baby—it's just a lot bigger!)

When we feed the calf for the first time, we try to give her two bottles of this milk. Then we feed the calf one bottle of colostrum twice a day for three days.

21

I'm filling up a few buckets with the powdered milk mix. We've got a lot of calves to feed.

After this, we don't feed the calf its mother's milk anymore. We feed the calf a powdered milk mix. To make the mix, we put two scoops of powdered milk into a bucket. Then we fill it with warm water and stir it really well. We make the mix twice a day. Mom and I feed the calves in the morning, and Kacie and I take over at night.

At the same time we start feeding the calf the mix, we feed it a **grain starter.** The grain starter is food made from mostly cracked corn with molasses mixed in for sweetness. The back of a calf's mouth has sharp teeth on the bottom and the top. When the calf eats, it grinds the corn with its teeth. The calf looks like it's chewing gum!

This is what the grain starter looks like close-up.

Kacie and I work together to feed our calves. They look hungry today!

When I'm not feeding the calves, I like to talk to them and make sure they're comfortable.

After two months, we put the calf on a regular diet of grain and water—no more milk mix. If we gave it more milk, we would overfeed it. Too much milk is not healthy for calves.

When the calf is about thirteen months old, Dad breeds her. She'll be almost two years old when her baby is born. After she gives birth, she can start to make milk.

Happy Cows Make Good MILK

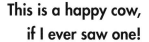
This is a happy cow,
if I ever saw one!

If a cow eats healthy food and is comfortable, she'll make milk. Dad feeds our cows a special mix four times a day. To make this food, he starts with a mix of grains and vitamins. Then he adds ground-up corn, chopped hay, and barley. (We grow this food on our farm.) This mixture is very good for our cows.

Our cows eat and sleep in a **free-stall barn.** In this barn, there are 320 stalls, or places to stand in. But the cows are not tied up in them. They are free to move around, lie down, and eat whenever they like. The main floor of the barn is covered with a rubber mat, so it's soft for the cows to stand on. Each stall has sand bedding that the cows seem to like a lot, too.

In the free-stall barn, our cows hang out and do what they like.

The electric fans in our barn really keep the cows cool when it's too hot for comfort.

Since cows don't like stuffy air, we have electric fans in the barn. These help to keep it cool during the warm months. All four sides of the barn and the ceiling are covered with chicken wire, so fresh air flows through. We play music for our cows, too. We know the happier our cows are, the more milk they make—and that's the truth!

I like to tease and play
with some of the cows.

By eating good feed, our cows
stay healthy and strong.

We milk our cows at 4 in the morning, noon, and 7:30 at night. Most days, our workers take turns milking. But every other weekend, I do the milking myself with other members of my family. For every milking, it takes about four hours to milk the cows.

The place where we milk our cows is called the **milking parlor.** It's connected to the free-stall barn, so it's easy for the cows to get to. The parlor is a big room with twenty-four stalls. (Each stall holds one cow.) The stalls are split into two rows, with twelve stalls in each.

These cows are waiting to be milked. It won't be long now!

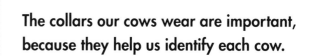

The collars our cows wear are important, because they help us identify each cow.

Our cows wear collars around their necks. Each collar has a computer chip on it. When the cows enter the parlor, their collars are scanned by a machine. This way, we know which cows are being milked.

Two workers then guide the cows to the milking machines. "Come on, girls," they say. The first cow turns slightly at one of the milking machines and puts its head over a bar. The second cow follows, until all twenty-four cows stand in the two rows of stalls. Before we start milking, all the collars are scanned again. This way, we can keep track of each machine and the cow it milks.

31

Below the cows is a four-foot deep pit. This is where workers stand while they get the cows ready and do the milking. Just before a cow is milked, a worker **strips** its four teats. The worker starts at the top of each teat. Then he gently squeezes the teat to get the first squirt of milk out. This helps the flow of milk to start.

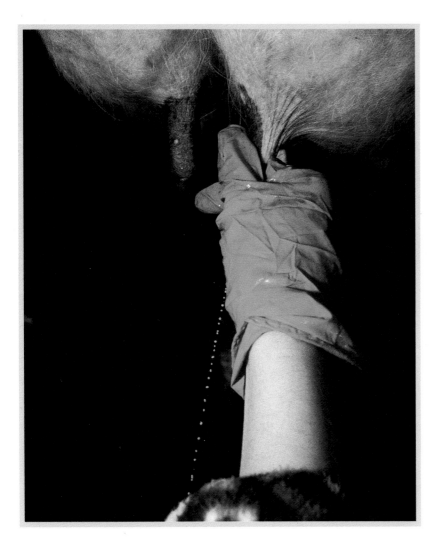

After the milk starts flowing, we can check the milk to make sure it's not lumpy. Stripping looks like it hurts the cow, but it doesn't.

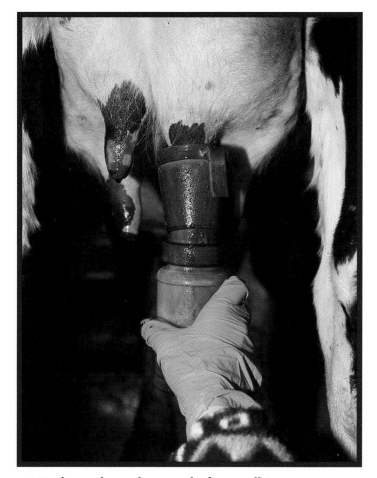 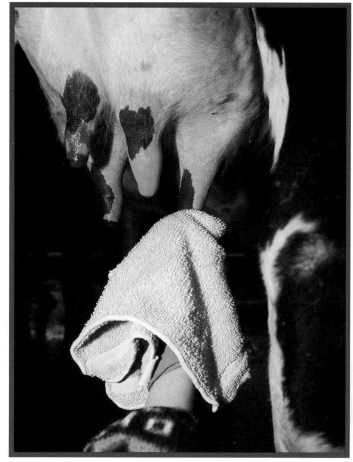

Workers clean the cow before milking.

After the worker strips the teats, he **dips** them into a special liquid that kills any germs. The liquid is in a small container that has a funnel-like top. The worker pushes this top up and over each teat.

About a minute later, a second worker wipes off the teats with a washcloth. Then he attaches a **milker** to them. (A milker is the part of the machine that milks the cows.) As soon as the milker is attached to the teats, it automatically starts to milk the cow.

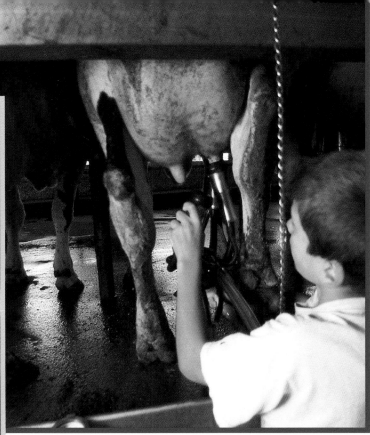

When it's milking time, I place suction cups on the cow's teats.

The milker has four suction cups, one for each teat. It's hooked up to a machine that pumps every second. Every time the machine pumps, it gently sucks milk from the udder. It doesn't hurt the cow at all. In fact, she's happy to have the milk taken from her full udder.

34

Each suction cup is attached to a hose. As the milk comes out of each teat, it goes through these hoses, then into a small container in the pit. From here, the milk flows through a pipeline, into a receiving jar in the nearby milk house. (The receiving jar looks like a giant jar.) Then a pump sucks the milk from the jar and takes it to a huge refrigerated tank. The tank cools the milk to between 36°F and 38°F. If the temperature is more than 38 degrees, the milk can't be used. The milk could be spoiled, and people can't drink spoiled milk. So we have to be very careful about temperature.

The receiving jar is above, and the refrigerated tank is on the right.

When a cow's milk stops flowing, the machine automatically shuts down. The milker drops from the teats. Then a chain that's attached to the milker pulls the milker out of the way. A computer in the pit shows how much milk each cow gives. It also tells how long it took to milk the cow (usually about ten minutes).

All of this information is stored in another computer. This way, we can keep track of each cow's milk production.

After twelve cows in one row have been milked, a worker opens the gate. Those cows leave the barn, and the next group comes in. Rows of cows come and go until all 400 cows are milked.

It's amazing to me how much milk we collect from our cows.

36

Mom looks at the computer sheets and checks to make sure our cows are giving enough milk.

Every month, a milk tester comes and takes a sample of each cow's milk. The milk is tested to make sure it is safe for people to drink. This is important, because we sell our milk to a **processing plant** that sells it to people. If a milk sample doesn't pass all the tests, the processing plant won't take it.

This is the milk tank that takes our milk away. It holds gallons and gallons of milk!

Every other day, a worker from the processing plant comes to pick up the milk. Before he takes it, he tests it again. If the milk is good, the worker loads the milk onto his truck. The truck has a big shiny tank on its back. It looks like a thermos on wheels and works like one, too. This thermos keeps the milk cool until it reaches the processing plant.

When the processing plant gets the milk, workers mix it, heat it, and add vitamin A, vitamin D, and calcium to it. More tests are done, too, to make sure the milk is safe to drink.

When the milk is ready, it's put into cartons and bottles. Then it's delivered to many different places, like your local grocery store. (That's where we buy ours!) I love milk and drink lots of it. I know it's good for my growing bones and muscles.

I drink three glasses of rich, cold milk every day.

I enjoy living on our dairy farm. I like the country, with its wide-open spaces and fresh air. And I especially like to work hard with my family. Since we have so much work to do, Kacie and I never get bored. When we're not working on the farm, we're going to school or doing our homework. But we have time for outside activities like rollerblading and riding our bikes, too.

In our spare time, Kacie and I like to play games together. We like to just hang out, too.

We love our cows.
But we also take time
to play and cuddle
with our cats.

I hope to take over the dairy farm someday, with Kacie's help. Even though we've learned a lot about running the farm, we'll probably take business courses in college. By then, Mom and Dad might be ready to take it easy. Running our farm is something I really look forward to!

Living on our farm is lots of work, but we really like it here. Plus, we have lots of fun!

Fun Facts about COWS

An average cow gives ninety glasses of milk a day. Some give 200,000 glasses of milk in a lifetime!

Milk is a rich source of calcium and protein, which help our muscles and bones grow strong.

DAIRY COWS GIVE US MILK AND OTHER PRODUCTS, SUCH AS ICE CREAM, CHEESE, AND BUTTER.

Cows don't usually live more than twenty years. In that time, a dairy cow can have as many as ten or twelve calves.

Cows eat about **80 pounds** of food a day.

After a cow eats, the food goes into her stomach. There, the food sticks together in lumps the size of tennis balls. These are called cud. The cow burps the cud up into her mouth. She chews and swallows it as many as 60 times! A cow can spend up to 8 hours a day chewing her cud.

COWS DRINK 25–50 GALLONS OF WATER EACH DAY— THAT'S ALMOST A BATHTUB FULL!

Cows love to eat cereal and potato chips!

A cow weighs between 1,200 and 1,400 pounds– that's ten to twenty-five times an average person's weight.

Learn More about COWS

Books

McDonald, Mary Ann. *Cows.* Chanhassen, MN: The Child's World, Inc., 1998. What are cow horns made of? Why are beef cattle raised? What are oxen? Covered with full-color photographs, this book explains many facts about cows and why they're so important to us.

Miller, Sara Swan. *Cows.* New York: Children's Press, 2000. This book describes the history of the cow and the life of a cow today. Find out what life is like on a dairy farm and how milk can be made into many kinds of foods, too.

Stone, Lynn M. *Cows.* Vero Beach, FL: Rourke Corporation, Inc., 1990. A great introduction to the cow, this book explains the characteristics of cows and where cows live. You'll also read about wild cows, baby cows, and dairy cows.

Websites

Breeds of Livestock
<http://www.ansi.okstate.edu/BREEDS/cattle>
Learn all about different breeds of cattle and other types of livestock. Also find answers to commonly asked questions about livestock.

Kids Farm
<http://www.kidsfarm.com>
Here's a site that was created by people who live on a Colorado ranch. Read about their life on the ranch and about all kinds of animals that live there. Learn about different animal sounds, farm equipment, and food that grows on the ranch. Have fun with crossword puzzles and coloring books, too.

Moomilk
<http://www.moomilk.com>
How well do you know cows? Take a cow quiz and find out! At this udderly cool site, you can learn about milk, try and win a creative cow contest, and print out yummy dairy recipes.

My Moo Cow Pages
<http://www.mymoocowpage.homestead.com>
This colorful site has lots of fun activities and information about cows. Learn "Moovelous" jokes, view favorite moo pictures, and read cow poetry. Visit Calf Corner and play games and puzzles, too.

GLOSSARY

breed: to make pregnant

bulls: male cattle

calve: the process of giving birth to a calf

calves: young cows or bulls

colostrum: the first milk a mother makes for her calf. This milk helps a calf to stay healthy.

dips: when a worker places a liquid on a cow's nipples to kill germs

free-stall barn: a barn where milking cows live

grain starter: a calf's first solid food. It is made from mostly cracked corn with molasses mixed in for sweetness.

heat: the time when a cow is ready to get pregnant

heifers: young cows that haven't given birth to a calf. Heifers can't give milk yet.

milker: a machine that automatically milks a cow

milking parlor: a room where cows are milked

mucus: a slippery coating that covers a newborn calf's body

strips: when a worker gently squeezes a cow's nipple to get the first squirt of milk out

teats: the small raised parts of a cow's belly through which a calf drinks milk

processing plant: a place where milk is tested and packaged

udder: the part of a cow that makes milk

veterinarian: an animal doctor

About the AUTHOR

Judy Wolfman is a writer and professional storyteller who teaches workshops on storytelling, creativity, and writing. She also enjoys writing and acting for the theater. She has published three children's plays, numerous magazine articles, short stories, poems, finger plays, and Carolrhoda's Life on a Farm series. A retired schoolteacher, Ms. Wolfman has two sons, a daughter, and four granddaughters. She lives in York, Pennsylvania.

About the PHOTOGRAPHER

David Lorenz Winston is an award-winning photographer whose work has been published by *National Geographic World,* UNICEF, and the National Wildlife Federation. In addition to his work on the Life on a Farm series, Mr. Winston has photographed farm animals for many years. He has also taught elementary school. In his spare time, he enjoys playing the piano at his home in southeastern Pennsylvania.